DISCARD

Peaceful Separation/ Peaceful Divorce

By HEATHER FRENNER, RYT
Chopra Yoga and Meditation Instructor

authorHOUSE®

AuthorHouse™
1663 Liberty Drive
Bloomington, IN 47403
www.authorhouse.com
Phone: 1-800-839-8640

© 2009 Heather Frenner, RYT, Chopra Yoga and Meditation Instructor. All rights reserved.

No part of this book may be reproduced, stored in a retrieval system, or transmitted by any means without the written permission of the author.

First published by AuthorHouse 4/22/2009

ISBN: 978-1-4389-7775-1 (sc)
ISBN: 978-1-4389-7774-4 (hc)

Library of Congress Control Number: 2009903615

Printed in the United States of America
Bloomington, Indiana

This book is printed on acid-free paper.

My compelling and successful journey of triumphant courage, woven with profound wisdom, will guide you daily in manifesting more peace, harmony, laughter, and love throughout your transition. Namaste!

I dedicate this book to my beloved daughter, Brittaney Lauren, who came into this world by the grace of two people who have the ultimate blessing and joy in being your parents. You are indeed the very salt of the earth and the bright and beautiful light of God. I am so very honored to be your mother, and I love you with all that I am.

I also dedicate this book to my precious dogs, Schatzi and Annie, who have never wavered—ever steady, ever true, always by my side.

To my beautiful equine friends, Annie, a gorgeous Belgium Draft (who recently transitioned), and Bruno, the ever-wild and spirited Mustang. You both helped set my spirit free!

I also, with the deepest respect and complete gratitude, dedicate this book to my beloved and cherished friend (of many lifetimes, for sure), Dr. Deepak Chopra, the greatest healer in the universe. You are the very essence of Christ Jesus and the incarnation of love itself.

To Dr. David Simon, superb author, physician, and medical director of the Chopra Center. Thank you for being my teacher. Your words of wisdom are profound. Learning from you felt like having Ghandi personally instruct me. I am honored.

To my wonderful parents, Sally and Ralph, who slipped into that eternal, non-local domain of everlasting peace six years ago. Thank you for raising me with only two rules: We do not use the H word (hate) and no war toys. You taught me that love is the ultimate gift of life.

To Robin Alexis, dear soul sister of mine. Thank you for your profound spiritual guidance and for helping me realize who I am and what I must accomplish on this earth. You are indeed authentic and a great light for all who are graced with your wisdom.

Also with beautiful appreciation and love for my dear friends Patrick Brauckmann, Dr. Charles Strole, Kelly Robert Hale, Paul Heussenstamm, Juan Miguel Avena, Nancy O'hanian, Alma Ordaz, Stephanie Ordaz and Sarah Ordaz, Samara Tricarico, Claire Diab, and each and every one of my treasured yoga and meditation students. Thanks especially to David Greenspan, Carolyn Rangal, and Teresa Long, who make the exquisite Chopra Center the ultimate nourishing experience for body, mind, and soul. Thank you for your never-ending guidance of love and support. I hold you, with grace and eternal love, forever in my heart.

To Phoebe Trachtenberg, my wonderful friend with the fine gift in editing. Your soft and gentle ways are refreshing, your ideas inspiring!

To the terrific staff of the City of Malibu, especially Molly Larson, Camille Gamboa and John Van Winkle. Your hard work and dedication are truly appreciated. You are amazing!

And, of course, I dedicate this book to my soon-to-be ex-husband, George. Thank you for the blessing of being married to you and for the sacred union that we shared in the exquisite creation of our greatest treasure, Britt.

To God. For You, with You and in You. Om Mane Padme Hum.

Preface

It can be done! You can absolutely manifest a peaceful and very harmonious separation and divorce. I have accomplished this through my training and personal experience.

Now, it is your turn! You can and deserve to be totally free from the stress that so very often accompanies a separation or divorce.

I will shepherd you with a very gentle and effective daily guide to achieving this outcome.

I am also very aware that each and every separation and divorce encompasses totally different dynamics and situations. Each relationship that ends in separation and divorce embodies a completely different set of polarities.

I feel that we must embrace these polarities of despair, with love, before we move on to the proven, healing advice given in this book. I do understand that it may be difficult to welcome the pain and agony of the hurtful actions inflicted on us, but until we take ownership of these actions, we will never be able to release them.

Believe me, I *know* what the dark and very ugly side of a toxic marriage feels like. I lived it, for many years.

I am also very grateful for the experience it brought to my awareness. I realized that there are thousands of individuals who are suffering in a toxic relationship and perhaps need to get out.

This book may be a wakeup call for some of you, signaling your need to leave an unhealthy relationship.

Right now, take out a piece of blank paper. Write down, in ink (as ink represents permanence), every single painful experience that you have endured with your partner. You may be as explicit as you would like, or as vague. The thing is to record everything that comes to your mind.

Next, close your eyes and try to relive, as much as you possibly can, these situations that came into your life. This process, as difficult as it seems, is very important for the next step.

You have now embraced these situations. Acknowledge them for what they are and realize why they came into your life.

Remember, these are situations and not the person. The individual acting out these situations is not the actual painful experience itself. Realize that they too are hurting and are not conscious of their actions, even when they are awake.

Take a deep breath in, embracing all of these situations and experiences, and release them as you slowly exhale.

Now, take this piece of paper filled with toxic emotion and discard it. You may tear it up, wrinkle it, or stomp on it, whatever feels best for you right now. Then dispose of it. Burn it in the fireplace, flush it down the toilet, throw it in the trash—however you choose, just get rid of it!

You do not own these situations anymore! Congratulations!

We each have our own story of being in a relationship that is not fulfilling, is not nourishing, and in some cases is very dangerous and life threatening.

We can get out of it with grace, with dignity, and with *love*. Trust in me and let me guide you now.

Love,
Heather

Introduction

Peace … harmony … laughter … love.

Is it possible? Can there really be a peaceful outcome in separating or divorcing one's betrothed?

Can harmony actually be achieved through the preconceived notion of, "You will be screwed if you don't do XYZ, and definitely do not forget to do *@*@!"

Can laughter really exist if we are going for their jugular vein?

Can love truly and wholeheartedly manifest when we are constantly on the lookout for our next move or next game plan in trying to make our future ex-spouse out to be the incarnated Judas Iscariot? What if we are trying to defend our fine, upright, puritan reputation of being the living example of Mother Teresa, Saint Joan of Arc, Mahatma Gandhi, or Saint Anthony of Padua?

Why is all of this happening to me? What could I possibly have done to manifest this situation? The quest begins. We begin to realize that we need to question why these very real situations are taking place in our lives and begin to even question reality as a whole and functioning part of our physiology. From family and friends, to colleagues and business partners, to churches and synagogues and houses of worship —and let us not forget our metaphysical friends, the soul sisters and brothers of yesteryear, and we simply cannot ignore our attorneys and mediation experts, who also put in their two cents, most definitely at an hourly rate!

Everyone involved with this very private matter means well. Their intentions are for our highest good, aren't they?

You seek endlessly for answers and guidance and support, constantly seeking, constantly looking for some type of direction. You need so very desperately for someone to throw you that magical rope, pulling you out of the turmoil, the anguish, and the strife.

Who can I trust? Who can I turn to? What is going to happen to me? What is going to happen to my children? What is going to happen to my pets? Will my friends and community reject me and my children?

Where is the security of the future?

Worry and fear set in, as well as sadness, depression, neglect, guilt, shame. It penetrates our body, it penetrates our mind, and eventually, it penetrates our soul. It gets in the way of our dharma, our soul's purpose, our journey—the very reason why we are here.

It is here, at the level of the soul, where we actually catch a glimpse of light before us—a faint and distant glow all the way down that dark corridor of loneliness. Yes, even though we have heard it a million times, there is indeed a beautiful and bright healing light, just waiting to transcend through us. It is guiding us gently to the next road, the future pathway to our next chapter in life, transitioning us to our own journey, a journey so very profound and so deeply nourishing.

The journey is that precious, illuminated pathway that leads us to that glorious, bright source. The source is indeed the light, which then manifests our own personal journey into beautiful healing.

Even though momentarily faint, this light will grow into the most lustrous prism of radiant love and is quite capable of illuminating the darkest cave, the darkest crevice, and the murkiest pathways.

Once you accept this and arrive at this perfectly divine level of consciousness, you are ready for the next step. So, go and get your broom! It is time to clear the cobwebs in your soul!

At this point, you have now accepted the fact that you are in this situation for a reason. The reason that this is happening to you right now, at this very moment in your life, is that you are being called to serve a higher purpose in life. Sometimes the most painful situations that we experience in life are just what is needed to bring us to that "A-ha!" moment in life, where we see a faint glimpse of light as the doors to our future pathways are gloriously revealed. It is here that we actually begin to experience the light, and it is here that we actually accept the light, with our body, mind, and soul.

This light *is* your very soul, the very essence of you. Your soul is pure light, pure radiance, pure love, and, most important pure potential.

In the profound self-realization that you are love and light, all that surrounds you will become a reflection of you, an infinite being of peace, harmony, laughter, and love.

You are the very essence of God, where the highest level of conscious awareness resides. It is here, at the level of the soul, where we begin to accept and embrace the conscious level of awareness in ourselves, in others, and in everything that surrounds us. We feel at one with the sacred reverence of life, because all of life is in us as we are in it. This is the purest form of potentiality. It is in this realm of consciousness, where we fully express our true potential of freedom—a freedom that does not place judgment or expectation on ourselves, other people, or situations that we are involved with. In this freedom, we actually harness pure potentiality, the friend of infinite possibilities. Everything *is* possible with God. This is that "A-ha!" moment that I mentioned earlier. We realize what *it* actually is. We realize what we are meant to do and what we are meant to become. This is our soul's journey. This is our purpose in life and it is why we are actually here living (and loving) on this earth.

Christ said, "I am in this world, and not of it." Let us pause here for a moment and contemplate this miraculous comment. You may wish to have someone read this next exercise to you as you close your eyes and surrender to the healing journey about to take place. Right now, wherever you are, please close your eyes. Begin to become aware of all that is surrounding your physical body. Physically notice the sounds surrounding your body, the sounds created by human actions, as well as the sounds manifested in nature. Do you hear cars going by? Do you hear the city bus or a country train? Is an airplane or helicopter flying overhead? Perhaps you are blessed with the sweet, innocent voices of children laughing in a playground. Or maybe you hear lovers giggling with delight in their newly discovered love for one another as they walk by on a glorious nature trail, filled with the first spring flowers. Perhaps you may hear the content sounds of dogs and horses embracing the polarities of their differences and living in union and bliss with one another as the twilight caresses the rising moon. Now, bring your awareness closer to your own integral being. Do you hear the breeze gently rustling through the trees or the ocean waves gently caressing the sand as the tide rolls in? Do you hear the sun's warmth as he kisses the first morning dew drops on the blooms of the morning glories? Perhaps you hear the birds chanting their melodic hymns as sunrise greets the new day. Do you hear the fog rolling in with the tide as the harvest moon shines all of her magnificence on the sea turtles? Is it possible for you to hear the amazing flittering of the wings of a monarch as it gently perches on the wild French lavender living carefree in your garden, or the gentle lull of the hummingbird enjoying the sweet nectar from the oranges blossoms, born of the magnificent grove of trees, with roots firmly living in the very earth you walk on? This is tranquility, and you are now, at this very moment in time, living the very essence of tranquility.

Now, gently and effortlessly release these sounds and bring this tranquility of awareness into your body. Listen to the sound of your breath, the most important part of your union with the divine. Our breath mirrors our thoughts, which has a direct correlation with the cellular functioning of our physiology. Physically witness the miracle of your breath as it unites your body with your mind and your soul. With each precious inhalation, feel your breath originate from your solar plexus (where personal power resides) and then slowly move your breath up into your chest (where you send love out into the world, and likewise, receive it back into your own integral being). Then, bear witness to your very powerful, healing breath as it shifts its energy all the way up into your throat (your region of personal expression). Please hold this breath. Hold onto this inhalation deeply inside of your throat and ask yourself, "What part of my separation and divorce do I need to release? What part of this situation is no longer serving me with peace, harmony, laughter, and love? How can I truly free myself from the bondage of judgment and of expectation?"

When you have this picture firmly planted in your mind, slowly and ever so gently release your breath, exhaling deeply into your throat, lowering your jaw, relaxing your tongue, releasing the tension in your eyebrows. Let it all go; feel the power of relinquishing everything that does not serve you in any way. Let your exhalation transcend down from your throat, bringing a serene calmness into your chest (your heart center).Finally, finding acceptance and completeness, allow your solar plexus to rise as it makes room for your breath to fulfill its intention of relaxation in the expansion of conscious awareness. Compress all of your breath here, in this region of personal power. Hold this exhalation. Please ask yourself, "What do I need to accept as a part of my healing journey from my separation and divorce? How can I transform this pain into beautiful and pleasurable moments of profound self-discovery? Most important, where is the light in this situation?" Then, slowly inhale and relinquish all judgment and fear. Gift yourself with the precious breath of acceptance, knowing that everything is in divine and perfect order right now.

Please repeat silently, "I am in this world and not of it. I am in this world and not of it. I am in this world and not of it." These are very powerful and truly beautiful words of the profound wisdom of Jesus Christ. When he spoke these words, the message that he conveyed was that we are indeed living and breathing human beings, inhabiting the earth, but our true self, our soul, is infinite, is carefree, and is love itself. As infinite human souls, we are the highest form of peace, living in harmony, having a lighthearted sense of laughter, and are totally and completely united in conscious bliss and love. We then become at one with everyone and everything around us, totally and completely incapable of manifesting harm to ourselves, other people, or anything that surrounds us, which is all of life and earth.

We are all beings of light and of love. Therefore, to cause harm or to judge someone or place expectations on someone or some situation is to not only inhibit their purpose of love and of light, but our own, as well. The very moment we cause another soul pain and discomfort, we simultaneously wreak havoc on our own soul's purpose and journey, and we take with us all of those precious souls that surround us, down that tumultuous journey of hell. Who needs this?

Once again, the sooner that we obtain realization of this concept, we can manifest change.

Mahatma Gandhi was so very accurate when he said, "We must be the change we want to see in the world." We can actually become the physical change that we want manifested in conscious reality. And, what is reality?

Reality is to become consciously aware of our greater purpose and our interconnectedness with one another through the exchanging of peace, harmony, laughter, and *love*.

You, my precious reader, are now harmonizing every cell in your body, every thought in your mind, and activating that sacred inner light (your soul) with these exquisite and powerful heart sutras of the great yogic sage, Patanjali.

Let us explore.

What does peace mean to you? What is peace? How does peace actually feel? Peace is being in a perpetual state of bliss, even in the midst of the most turbulent of storms. The integral part of our soul, which is the realm of light and the direct source of love, actually detaches from any form of chaos and havoc. You enter a state of conscious awareness that resides in love rather than fear. We can access this state of unified bliss through the regular practice of meditative activities, such as yoga and meditation. Prayer is essential, as well. It has been said that when we pray, we talk to God, and when we meditate, God talks to us. Through these practices, we simultaneously choose situations that serve us, and all of those precious souls that surround us, with peaceful responses, which manifest into peaceful outcomes that are nourishing. We become immune to criticism. We repel judgment and expectation and no longer seek the approval of others. Most important, we do not accept hatred into our lives and will absolutely not permit hatred to enter the lives of those who depend on us. We become the tranquility that we seek, which then leads us into harmony.

What does harmony mean to you? What is harmony? How does harmony feel?

Harmony is to feel good about ourselves and of our actions. To feel good about the way we live. To feel good about the way we treat other people and animals. To feel good about our own personal impact on the earth and her environment. To truly, wholeheartedly feel a nourishing sense of our being. This is harmony—a union with ourselves and everything and everyone that surrounds us, in a harmonious way. Harmony can be achieved, as it the very essence of our thoughts, which then physically govern our actions, which eventually govern our cellular function. If we take the time to engage in wholesome, nourishing activities, such as meditation and yoga, we will experience less stress in our everyday lives. Stress is the obstacle of our intentions and desires and is the direct opposite feeling of harmony. When we experience stress, depending on what type of stressful situation we encounter, certain regions or energy centers located along our spine (also known as chakras) tend to close as a natural way to defend ourselves. With the closure of these energy centers, the blood coagulates and skin cells become sticky. Together this forms a mass. This mass, which thrives on stress, is known as *ama* in the profoundly healing ayuravedic medical practice. Ama has the potential to manifest itself into a full-blown disease. What is disease? Dr. Deepak Chopra describes it purely as *dis-ease*. We are simply not at ease with ourselves, those in our lives, or even the environment in which we live. We are in charge of this! First, let us begin by not taking everything in life so seriously. We need to find the humor in situations and in ourselves. We need to laugh real laughter, right from the gut! Laughter is healing, in and of itself. It has the power to make us feel good. It has the power to harmonize our thoughts and our actions, which then takes us into the third component of the heart sutras of Patanjali.

Laughter. What does laughter mean to you? What is laughter, really? How does laughter feel?

Laughter means to look at life and life situations and people with a light-hearted sense of humor. We are not laughing *at* someone or *at* something. Rather, we are laughing *with* people and *with* situations and also *with* ourselves. We are not perfect. We do make mistakes. "Let he without sin cast the first stone." More profound wisdom from Jesus Christ. If we can embrace this concept with a light-heartedness and a feeling of humor, we can actually harmonize our thoughts and feelings. We release toxic emotions and let go of judgment and expectations. We grace ourselves with the freedom of acceptance. This acceptance releases the negative impact of stress in our lives and nourishes our very being. We fall in love with the pure essence of ourselves. Finally, what *is* love?

What does *love* mean to you? What really is love? What does love feel like?

> "To love is not a part of things
> or a part of life.
> To love is the whole of things
> and the whole of life.
> In my heart is my love for you
> and in my love for you
> life whole is."

This beautiful and exquisite poem (author unknown) exemplifies the complete love of self. It encompasses the total union of body, mind, and spirit. It invokes the purest of all feelings and emotions, totally healing and nourishing every cell in our bodies. Ah, yes, love. Not a mere four-letter word but a feeling—a feeling so vast, so miraculous, that it transcends everything that enters its path. It transports all people, all situations and circumstances to that precious journey of grace. Eventually, each and every one of us will reach that inevitable part of our lives where nothing else matters but *love*. For love is what it really is all about. It is the very reason why we are here: to learn *how* to love one another. "Here, by the grace of God, go I." Love teaches us acceptance. Love teaches us forgiveness. Love teaches us patience and grace and the wisdom we need in learning tolerance. Love is the most healing vibration we give to ourselves and to all of those who surround us. Love is God intoxicating our soul with nourishment and bliss. There simply is nothing more fulfilling, nothing more complete. When we feel God's passion of light living inside of us, we radiate this light to the universe. We become peace, we become harmony, we become laughter, and we become love. We become the light of God.

When I die, the world will be silent about me, keeping behind only one word: I have loved.

Rabindranth Tagore

How To Use This Book

The words of wisdom found in this book are intended to be your daily source of inspiration, gently guiding your body and nourishing your soul toward a beautiful path of peace, harmony, laughter, and love. Each chapter contains the necessary components to manifest positive karmic action during the transition of separation and divorce. When you make the conscious choice to follow the guided chapters, your intentions and desires will unfold quite naturally and manifest into the field of infinite possibilities of the purest potentiality.

The following chapters are intended for deep reflection, and I ask you to please only read one chapter a day. I understand that many of you will want to delve into the next chapter, but please, simply allow each precious chapter to resonate nourishment and healing. We are not in a rush to obtain enlightenment. We will gradually begin to not only see a difference in our lives, but to feel it, think it, and live it. We will become the change that we want to have fulfilled.

Please begin reading the first chapter on a Sunday, and conclude with chapter seven on the following Saturday. You may then wish to continue reading each chapter over and over again, in the previous manner. It will become a source of inspiration and strength. These chapters, over the course of one week, will change your life forever.

They are profound, and I assure you, they will transport your body, your mind, and your soul on an exquisite journey into healing.

These chapters also reflect the very essence of the remarkable book *The Seven Spiritual Laws of Success*, written by Dr. Deepak Chopra. When we apply these principals to our separation and divorce, a peaceful resolution will arise out of the confusion, turmoil, and hideous chaos. Harmony will take the place of havoc. Laughter will manifest rather than arguments, and most important, hatred will be conquered by the greatest settlement of all: *love*.

Enjoy!

Love and many blessings,

Heather

By the way, please visit www.Chopra.com at some point during your transition of separation and divorce. You will find nourishing food for thought and join with millions of likeminded individuals who are seeking to live a more harmonious way of life. "Journey into Healing" is one course that I would highly recommend.

Chapter One: Sunday

Daily affirmation to tear out and carry with you throughout your day:

I grace myself with silence, witnessing the beauty and love in myself and in all living things.

Sunday

The wisdom for today reflects the feeling of being absolute, of being non-judgmental, and of appreciating all of the magnificence found in nature, our refreshing oasis and the true healing source.

A transition from being married (till death do us part) into a separation and/or divorce truly does not need to be a death, but a gentle parting of sweet joy and unbounded bliss. If you completely surrender to the level of the soul and allow universal spirit to transition through your soul, which is also infinitely connected with the soul of your soon-to-be ex-spouse, you will find the freedom to love him or her in a new, profoundly enlightened way. It is in this discovery of freedom, in this enlightened state of love, where we access the level of the soul, which is the source of true power; it is who we really are, an infinite being who loves all and *is* all with one. The human soul, quite simply put, would never, ever cause pain and suffering to another soul, because that other soul is the mirror, that sacred, divine reflection of our own soul. I am sure you have heard family, friends, colleagues, and even strangers compliment you on your appearance. It makes us feel beautiful and accepted and appreciated and even more apparent. The compliment is mirroring not only our thoughts and our actions and the way we feel about ourselves, but the compliment in and of itself is the direct reflection of the person who is complimenting you! Our souls are the very reflection of love itself. And, our true self, which is our soul, *is* unbounded and carefree and filled with infinite love and light. When we learn to live a life based on love, we bring into our life, and the lives of all of those who surround us, wholesome and nourishing relationships based on non-judgment and non-expectation. This is the realm that the soul thrives in. This is the field of pure potentiality.

How do we access the power of our true self and embrace that sacred realm for our soul to thrive in as we go through separation and divorce? We access it by taking time today to grace ourselves with silence, taking time to enjoy all of the beauty and wonder of the universe. We access it by not judging or expecting anything from anyone or any situation. We access it by appreciating the gift of life and love in our lives, and we begin the miraculous journey. We begin to manifest change.

How to manifest the change you would like to see in your separation and/or divorce:

A.) Truly become silence. Take some time today to quiet your body, your mind, and your soul by taking some time for yourself, silently. Literally, gift yourself with silence. We give so much of ourselves by giving our time that we often neglect to take the time to replenish our own integral being to simply *be*. Even in the midst of chaos and turmoil, we are still capable of accessing harmony. If your partner has anger and manipulation and control issues (as they so often do in separation and divorce cases), your silence will actually let you become immune to criticism and immune to fear. You will have accessed your soul in this silent replenishment of acceptance.

Your true divine source of power will harness the calm serenity that lies deep within your soul. Please be gentle with yourself and honor your soul by gifting your body and mind with the precious blessing of silence. You will find that meditation is simply the finest way to observe silence and harness pure potentiality, which will bless you with infinite possibilities of peace, harmony, laughter, and love. Give yourself the gift of meditation at least twice a day for about a half an hour each time, preferably at sunrise and at sunset, and watch the benefits grow!

B.) Take a hike! Detach from the drama of your soon-to-be ex-spouse and go for a walk in nature. Nature has very powerful, healing energies just waiting to nourish your senses. As you physically connect with the earth, you connect with the universal spirit. Bear witness to the miraculous creations of God. Become one with yourself, through all living things.

C.) "Judge ye not" is the key function today. Please remind yourself not to judge anyone or any situation, including yourself. I know this might be difficult as your soon-to-be ex-spouse may be pissing you off. Hey, we are only human. You say your soon-to-be ex-spouse is not in *your* space of love and is engaging in acts of judgment, expectation, and even hatred? Let us recall those very poignant words of Jesus Christ. "Let he who is without sin cast the first stone." Don't go looking for the hugest rock you can find to hurl at your personal pain-in-the-ass! Acknowledge that you are angry and *move on*! When we acknowledge our feelings and detach from the drama, we enter the space of acceptance, which is the foundation of love. Embrace hatred with love! The more love we bring into this situation, the less we judge. The more we judge others, the more we judge ourselves and the more others judge us. It is really a vicious circle of soul biting and gnawing! It is so much easier to relinquish all thoughts of judgment and enter that divine principal of *Namaste*, where you actually honor the divine in them, as they honor the divine in you.

The spiritual essence of today activates the seventh chakra, also known as the sahasrara chakra or crown chakra. It is located at the top of the head and is envisioned as a magnificent, thousand-petal lotus blossom, opening directly upward, toward the heavens, directly linking our soul to God, to all there is, to universal spirit. This chakra is embraced by the glorious color of violet, which encompasses all religions and all forms of spirituality. The universal sound that activates this chakra is the sound of creation itself. It is *om*. Please take a moment to sit silently, in a cross-legged position, if comfortable. Close your eyes and take a deep breath in through your nostrils. Slowly and gently exhale the healing vibration, om.

There is also a lovely and restorative yoga posture, also known as *asana*, that activates this crown chakra. It is a glorious posture known as Matsyasana, the fish pose. It will offer an extension into a more complete and full breath, as it releases built-up tension from the pelvic region. It also will benefit the thyroid gland. As with common sense, please consult the advice of a physician before engaging in any of the yoga poses instructed in this book.

Lie flat on your back. Then, bend both knees as you rest both feet on the floor, slightly wider than hip width apart, with your toes pointed slightly inward. Next, gently roll your right hip upward as you bring your right arm underneath the right side of your body, with the right palm turned down. Then, lower the right hip down, on top of your right arm. Repeat this procedure on your left side. Next, extend your left leg straight out and rest it on the floor. Repeat this same procedure with your right leg, and point the toes on both feet. Please now begin to fill your lungs with a deep inhalation of breath as you allow your chest to rise up and off of the floor. Let your head gently focus on a beautiful place behind, as you rest the top of your head on the floor. Glide the tip of your tongue along the roof of your mouth until it reaches the top two front teeth. Close your eyes and breathe. Become one with your breath and let your body release all anxiety into this pose. When you are ready to come out of it, inhale and simply raise your head and shoulders; then exhale as you slowly bring your chin to your chest. Inhale and slowly lower your shoulders and head back to the floor. Release your arms from underneath you and rest with legs straight out in front of you, arms out to the side. Breathe.

Photograph by Jasper Johal

"MATSYASANA FISH POSE"

And now I shall leave you for the day with an absolutely exquisite poem, written by the amazing Bengali poet Rabindranth Tagore. Enjoy.

This Is My Delight

This is my delight, to watch and wait by the wayside,
As the shadow races the light
And the summer rain chases the sun.
Messengers greet me from unknown skies
Racing past on the road.
My heart is glad, the passing breeze is sweet,
Because I know that in one moment
I will see.

Meanwhile I sit before my door
Smiling and singing alone.
Meanwhile the air is filling with sweet perfume
Of promise.

Self-Reflection Page

Please take a moment as you retire for the evening. Sitting comfortably in your bed, begin to journal your day. How was your day? How are you feeling physically, emotionally, and spiritually, right now? Let us begin the beautiful process of recapitulation. Remember, the joy is the very journey itself. Namaste.

Chapter Two: Monday

Daily affirmation to tear out and carry with you throughout your day:

I am the very essence of *love*, and *love* is the very essence of *me*.

Monday

The wisdom for today reflects complete love: love for self and a love for others; a love for the environment and all living things. The more love we give in life, the more love we will receive. And the more we appreciate life's blessings, the more we open the direct channel of abundance to flow harmoniously into our lives and all of those precious lives that surround us.

How on earth is it possible to give love when we feel the excruciating, heart-wrenching pain and anger, triggered by a separation and/or divorce? How can we receive love and a feeling of harmony when it is quite obvious that our soon-to-be ex-spouse is trying to manipulate us with hateful actions? These are very real questions that some of my students, who are going through the transition of separation and into divorce, approach me with. Their feelings are deeply heartfelt, profoundly valid, and so very real. It moved me to the point where I felt compelled to write this book. I know that when I was personally going through this process, I was not able to find a single written resource on the topic of peaceful separation/peaceful divorce. So, the healing project of writing began. I realized that what I have come to learn through my own experiences in life and my own self-realization—and also through obtaining invaluable insight and wisdom from some of the world's greatest healers of mind/body health—was something that needed to be shared with humanity. Not only for those afflicted with the pain of separation and divorce, but for all of those precious individuals (including the lawyers and mediation experts) who surround those individuals going through separation/divorce.

If we pause for just a moment and think about the seed (bija in sanskrit) of pain, anger, disgust, and hatred, we will find the direct source, which is FEAR.

Frighten (to drive something away by terrorizing)

Erratic (haphazard, desultory, and spasmodic actions)

Attack (to set upon with force)

Rebellion (resisting love and having desire to fight)

Fear is the source of all acts of violence and hatred. Fear arises from a feeling of being frightened. We somehow have given power to a feeling that we will be attacked, which can be very frightening, indeed. We feel that the erratic, rebellious acts of vindictive behavior will swallow us alive in the complete and utter terror of fright itself.

Many years ago, a very dear friend of mine told me something that completely changed my outlook on life. This simple sentence had the power to manifest the healing vibration of acceptance. She said, "Rejection is God's protection." That was all she said. When she died, I promised myself that I would somehow get her simple words out into the universe, to offer a bit of comfort, a bit of nourishment, and a feeling that all is as it should be. Everything is indeed in perfect and divine order. Those very poignant words, spoken well by my friend, exemplified consciousness, embracing an understanding awareness of what fear really is. Fear is merely a form of rejection. When we begin to accept rejection with love, we begin to detach from what it is that does not serve us and our general well-being. It places us in the palms of God's loving hands of divine protection. With this reassurance that everything is actually in divine and perfect order, right now, we then open a gateway of love. We then are able to sow the seeds of love where once hatred was attempting to pollute our soul. Love then detoxifies those seeds of hatred and replaces that grotesque energy with harmony. We then nourish the universe and allow the universe to nourish us through the acceptance of peace and harmony and laughter and love.

Love (ultimate gift of God)

Omniscient (having infinite awareness, understanding, and insight)

Verisimilitude (state of being real)

Everlasting (never ending)

When we are in a state of love, our life reflects bliss. We are engaged in conscious acts of loving that resonate an omniscient state of verisimilitude, a pure place of living a truthful life and of being real, of being authentic. Leading a life with authenticity is everlasting and shall endure, even in the most turbulent of waters.

By relinquishing the posterity of fear, we actually harness the seeds of love. Likewise, if we permit fear to manipulate our life, we sabotage any form of love that is trying to exist. Picture this: spring is coming and a new flower is about to emerge from that sacred seed that was planted deeply into the earth. The sun shone on this seed, warming it, preparing it, nourishing it. Rain quenched the seed's thirst for life. The earthworms tilled the soil. Oxygen from giant deciduous trees permeated the space, surrounding the seed, making way for the expansion of growth. The seed took its first breath of life and became a seedling, sprouting its way up into the arms of the sun's glorious embrace, full with the anticipation of life itself, of infinite possibilities and unbounded bliss. The sheer moment of creation being born into pure potentiality. Yet if the sun never did shine and environmental conditions did not permit clouds to manifest those precious droplets of water, the earthworms would shrivel up and die. The seed would never grow. The same holds true if we are closed up in the agony and sorrow of fear. The manifestation of love will simply never exist. Hence, if we are blocking the healing energies trying to emerge from within, we will never give life to that precious seed that lies deep within our soul. Seeds simply cannot flourish without love.

Let *love* be your seed today.

The spiritual essence of today activates the fourth chakra, also known as the anahata chakra. It is located in the center of the chest, where love actually resides. It is the place where we send love out into this bright and glorious universe, and where we receive it back into our own integral being of body, mind, and spirit. This is the sacred space where all of love originates in us. It is where love pours out of us and into the universe, and it is where we embrace the universal shower of love's hydration, bringing it back into our own integral being. The beautiful color of a bright and vibrant emerald green forest radiates from within this chakra. The universal sound that activates this chakra is *yam*. Please take a moment to sit silently in a comfortable and cross-legged position, if possible. Close your eyes and take a deep breath in through your nostrils. Slowly and gently exhale the healing sound, *yam*.

There is also a lovely and restorative yoga asana to activate the anahata chakra. It is known as the butterfly pose or Baddha Konasana. As with common sense, please consult the advice of a physician before engaging in any of the yoga poses instructed in this book. Begin by sitting on the floor and gently bring the soles of the feet together. Caress the toes with the palms of your hands. Sitting up straight and tall, tip the pelvis down. Gently relax your head and shoulders. Then, slowly lower your head toward your feet. Close your eyes and transcend into this pose, allowing your breath to soothe your mind into a tranquil state of bliss. Your head will naturally gravitate toward your feet, inch by inch, vertebra by vertebra. Inhale deeply and then exhale as you slowly come back up into a seated position. Your head and shoulders are the very last to come up. Next, in the same seated position, gently hold your toes with your left hand and place your left elbow and forearm on the floor, directly in front of your left shin. Gently press the right thigh down to the floor and lower your right shoulder as you extend your right arm out and up towards the ceiling. When you find a comfortable stretch, expand your breath by bringing your entire right arm back a few inches. Open the fingertips of your right hand as much as possible and bring the thumb and index finger (which is associated with the heart chakra, your anahata chakra) together, placing the thumb directly over the lowered index finger, forming a very beautiful and powerful hand mudra (the yoga of the hands), known as Vayu Mudra. Glide your tongue along the roof of your mouth to the area right in front of your top two front teeth. Transcend into this pose through your breath. When you are ready to come out of this pose, inhale deeply; then exhale as you lower your right arm back down. Repeat this procedure on your other side, taking all the time you need to engage in the pose and to come out of it. We are not in a rush for enlightenment here, so please take your time. When you have stretched both sides beautifully, please enjoy the beginning part of this sequence by simply letting your head come down to your feet. You will notice that this time, your head will naturally come down a little bit farther. The benefits of yoga are instantaneous, as when your meet your beloved for the first time and realize that you have been with him or her forever.

Photograph by Jasper Johal

"BADDHA KONASANA BUTTERFLY POSE"

I will now leave you with this magnificent poem by the thirteenth-century sufi poet, Rumi.

The Meaning of Love

Both light and shadow
Are the dance of love.
Love has no cause;
It is the astrolabe of God's secrets.
Lover and loving are inseparable
And timeless.
Although I may try to describe Love
When I experience it I am speechless.
Although I may try to write about Love
I am rendered hopeless;
My pen breaks away and the paper slips away
At the ineffable place
Where Lover, Loving and Loved are One.
Every moment is made glorious
By the Light of Love.

Self-Reflection Page

Please take a moment as you retire for the evening. Sitting comfortably in your bed, begin to journal your day. How was your day? How are you feeling physically, emotionally, and spiritually, right now? Let us begin the beautiful process of recapitulation. Remember, the joy is the very journey itself. Namaste.

Chapter Three: Tuesday

Daily affirmation to tear out and carry with you, throughout your day:

My heart is my best guide. It will direct me in every choice that I make, manifesting the best possible outcome for me and for all of those precious individuals who surround my world.

Tuesday

The wisdom for today is reflective of the choices that we make. Choices manifest into direct action. If we pause and take the necessary time that we need when making our choices, we then create an action that will bring fulfillment and happiness to ourselves, to all of those individuals who surround us, and eventually, to our actions. We literally have the power to make a difference in the world by simply making the most peaceful, harmonious, light-hearted choice, which will bring love into each and every situation that we encounter!

"Whoa, baby. That is where you lost me!" a friend of mine told me recently. As he continued to complain about the high cost of attorneys' fees (adding that one of his friends spent about $800,000 on just his lawyer alone), he wondered how on earth things got this bad. With all due respect to our legal professionals (and we certainly do need you), quite frankly, some of you act as if it is your birthright to take two people who have made the choice to split and magnify this molehill into a huge mountain of utter chaos, confusion, and hatred.

There is nothing more important today than to embrace our differences with acceptance. We need to step out of the proverbial ego and make our actions reflect peace, harmony, laughter, and love. We need to act rather than react to the sudden outbursts of anger, which are only fear based. We explored fear in chapter two. So, let's move forward and not get caught in the momentary sand trap of time. Please remember, once an action has been created, it will be with us forever. We simply cannot take that action away. If your actions are made in haste and anger, you will allow the thoughtless judgment of others' opinions to rule *your* life. You will literally give your life to someone else to run! Likewise, if your actions are made with love, a peaceful, harmonious, and light-hearted outcome will follow. You have the ultimate power to choose the life you want. Why would you give this precious gift to someone else, who did not have the exact same experience as you and who truly does not know how you feel?

I remember a woman who was married twice. The first time she divorced her husband (in the sixties, a time of poetry, love, and Woodstock, reflecting the feeling "We have to set our differences aside and work together as one humanity"), she had a peaceful divorce. Sure, both individuals felt the pain of the process, but each had a profound understanding of respect and freedom. Perhaps, the environment of the sixties had a direct impact on their choices, as there clearly was more at stake here. The very theme of this era held an omnipresent aura, a psychedelic field of love. I even remember as a small child protesting the Vietnam War on my dad's shoulder's, chanting, "Make love, not war." It kind of became my childhood mantra! Where did the love stop?

When this same woman remarried, sure, she had bliss and all that followed. Eventually, she divorced her second husband, but, that divorce was a living hell, for her and for everyone around her. Children, pets, friends, family, even the plants in her garden—they *all* went into the repulsive sewer of hate. What was accomplished in these acts of hatred? Many years later, the confusion of lies and deceit still lingers in the wafting air of hatred that hovers above her head. She has even manifested illness from harboring massive resentment. It is really so sad. And for what? How could this beautiful woman go through two completely different divorces? I watched it all unfold, every step of the way. What I came to realize was that *she* had the ultimate choice in how each divorce manifested. Yes, she had the power to control every motive, every line in the script of each movie. With her first divorce, she remained in her heart center. With her second one, she gave her power over to the demands of hatred.

So, my precious readers, you have picked up this book for a reason. How will *you* choose to journey your road of separation and/or divorce? Will the choices you make today bring you peace? Will they bring you harmony? Will you laugh at your mistakes and of your soon-to-be ex-spouse's errors? Will your choices be made from your heart, bringing more love into your life?

Today, right now, make a commitment to create and manifest a peaceful outcome as you journey through separation and/or divorce. The following exercise will help to facilitate and ground you and will ultimately be your source of strength as you travel this road.

Find a lovely piece of white paper and an ink pen. Draw a vertical line down the center of the paper. On the left side, write down all of those situations of your separation/or divorce that are annoying you and bringing stress into your life. Next, close your eyes and see yourself living a life without all of these disturbances. Take a deep breath in, feeling a deep sense of relief, and exhale out all that which does *not* serve you any longer. Please open your eyes slowly and look at your list again. Circle the top three situations that need your immediate attention and write these three situations on the right side of the paper, giving enough space between the words. Now, beside each word make an = sign. Our action = our thoughts! Begin to think of all of the ways you can bring more peace, more harmony, more laughter (lighten up, man!) and more love into each of these three situations *today*. Then, simply make the commitment to follow through with your intentions in manifesting more peace, harmony, laughter, and love into your life! You are in control. You are in the driver's seat. Will you make the road you are traveling on smooth and straight or will it be filled with the potholes of despair? When your list is complete, hang it up, with conviction and strength, in a place where you will look at it often. Now, your seeds have been planted and, with proper care and maintenance, will blossom into the most harmonious flower of truth. Continue with this writing exercise every Tuesday, until the left side of your original list, which was filled with all of the stresses in your life, have been completely eradicated.

You are now living in peace. Your life will be filled with less stress, because you are now consulting your heart with all of the choices that you are making. You, my precious readers, are now embracing the future with the acceptance of peace, harmony, laughter, and love.

You have within you a beautiful and elegant light of etiquette and grace. Let this radiant light permeate every thought in your mind, gracing you with exquisite respect and dignity.

Be present.

The spiritual essence of today activates the first chakra, also known as the muladhara chakra or root chakra. It is located at the base of the spine, where we have basic survival issues and also where the fight/flight instinct was cognized. This chakra is embraced with a deep, rich, healing red color and has a magnificent healing sound of *lam*. Please take a moment to sit in a cross-legged position, if comfortable. Close your eyes and take a deep breath in, through your nostrils. Slowly and gently exhale the healing vibration *lam*.

There is also a beautifully restorative yoga posture known as Padmasana, the glorious lotus flexion. This pose has a very calming effect on the brain. It stimulates the pelvic joints, the spine, the abdomen, and the bladder. It stretches the knees and ankles. It eases menstrual discomfort and sciatica. Traditional texts state this pose will destroy all disease. As with common sense, please consult the advice of a physician before engaging in any of the yoga poses instructed in this book. Please begin by sitting on the floor with both of your legs straight out in front of you. Physically shift the flesh from both sides of your buttocks outward. Tip the pelvis up and then downward. Take your right foot and place it on top of your left thigh. Rest the right ankle as you massage the arch of your right foot. Next, if it is comfortable, bring your left ankle and rest it on top of your right thigh, massaging the arch of your left foot as you completely relax your left ankle. If this is not yet comfortable (once again, we are not in a rush for enlightenment here), simply rest your left ankle beneath your right thigh in what is known as the half lotus position. Next, still sitting in a comfortable upright position, please roll your shoulders up and then back down. This will expand your chest, and you will be able to make a more complete breath. Take your hands and place them in a prayer position as you rest them on your heart. Close your eyes and feel yourself becoming one with your breath. Silently witness the healing power of each inhalation and each exhalation.

Now, simply let go of all tension in your life and release this tension through your healing breath. All is as it should be, so *be*.

Photograph by Jasper Joh

"PADMASANA LOTUS FLEXION"

I will now leave you for the day with this lovely poem by Hafiz, a Persian poet in the Sufi tradition. Beneath the surface of his writings, one will find his emphasis on union with the divine, a sacred union with God. Enjoy.

Etiquette

How should two people treat each other
If they both know God?
Like a musician touching his violin
With utmost care
To caress the final note.

Self-Reflection Page

Please take a moment as you retire for the evening. Sitting comfortably in your bed, begin to journal your day. How was your day? How are you feeling physically, emotionally, and spiritually, right now? Let us begin the beautiful process of recapitulation. Remember, the joy is the very journey itself. Namaste.

Chapter Four: Wednesday

Daily affirmation to tear out and carry with you throughout your day:

I now accept all situations that enter my life, knowing that everything is in divine and perfect order right now. These exact situations bless me with the responsibility that I am gifted with, enabling me to be open to divine perspective and guidance.

Wednesday

The wisdom for today reflects complete and total acceptance. In accepting all situations, be they good or bad, I grace myself with the exquisite responsibility that I need at this point in my life. This new responsibility will bless me with the freedom to make the correct, spontaneous choice at any given moment in life. Knowing this, I may then be free from defending myself, as I now have a complete and total understanding that divine action is manifesting the best possible outcome for me and for all of those precious, infinite beings who surround me.

Please read the following paragraph first and then delve into the Freedom from Bondage exercise. Sitting comfortably with your eyes closed, take a beautifully deep, relaxing breath in, feeling the breath originate from the solar plexus region in your body. Totally fill the belly (the region of personal power) with your healing breath (also known as pranayam in the enlightening world of yoga). Then, shift that same healing inhalation into your chest (where love is received and then released), filling the lungs completely. Then, with that same exact inhalation, shift this powerful, healing breath into the region of your throat (the region of personal expression) and *hold it*. Physically hold onto this same inhalation until it becomes uncomfortable.

Now, ask yourself, "What part of my separation/divorce am I still holding on to?" When you cannot hold onto this inhalation any longer, release your breath, slowly releasing in your mind that part of your separation and divorce that you need to detach from as your powerfully healing breath takes it away from your mind. Send it back down through your chest and release it in the solar plexus region. Feel the complete and total acceptance this just brought to your body, your mind, and your soul. How wonderful your soul feels now that it does not need to carry around that emotional baggage anymore!

Now, at the same time, take a lovely breath in, using the same manner as before. When your breath has reached your throat, simply release it. Send that exhalation back down through your chest and release it all the way down into the solar plexus. Physically exhale every bit of breath out of you and then *hold it*. Hold that exhalation until it becomes uncomfortable. Now ask yourself, "What part of my separation/divorce do I need *accept* with dignity and with respect?" When you feel that you cannot hold onto this exhalation any longer, inhale. Inhale the prana, the life, the precious part of the acceptance that you need to be *free*. Pause for a moment, with deep appreciation and gratitude for everything that is in your life. How gorgeous your soul must be feeling right now, at this very moment in time, after accepting only the wholesome nourishment of your separation/divorce. Yes, you *did* hear me correctly. Separation and divorce *can* be deeply wholesome and profoundly nourishing because you made a conscious choice to release *all* of that which does not serve you any longer, and you have consciously made the choice to replace it with the acceptance of *everything* that will serve you, in a beautiful and harmonious manner..

Acceptance brings glorious responsibility, which brings infinite possibilities of the purest potentiality. If we make a conscious choice to seize the moment, we transform every single problem into the most awesome opportunity. It's true. Believe me. I am living proof.

We all tend to hold onto ridiculous situations that are painful and totally and completely not intended for us. Many people simply numb themselves in order to cope. They numb themselves by detaching from their feelings and hide those feelings in alcohol, drugs, overeating, or some other form of self-destructive behavior. After having my marriage blessed in the Catholic Church, that is precisely what I did. I was so very unhappy in my marriage (yet felt that it would be the greatest sin in the universe if I even *thought* about separation and divorce), so rather than confronting my emotional discomfort, I numbed myself on Girl Scout cookies—Thin Mints, to be exact. I numbed myself so much that I went from being a six-foot-tall former runway model, a perfect size six, into being this two hundred and twenty-five pound woman! I could not believe that I could even allow this to happen. So, the universe *blessed* me with a major problem. What I now have come to deeply appreciate and embrace wholeheartedly is the opportunity it gave me. It took my husband having an affair, and me releasing him and his mistress with complete acceptance and truly wishing them infinite joy of peace, harmony, laughter, and love! And, I meant it! For as soon as I did this, I got my old figure back again, only this time with a major shift: enlightenment! I became a Chopra yoga and meditation instructor and developed an amazing and truly beautiful clientele. I began writing this book (three years in the making), and most important, gave my greatest blessing in life, my precious, precious daughter, the wisdom of *empowerment*. I graced my family with love and embraced my husband's family with deep appreciation and infinite friendship. I also made it quite clear to all of those precious and sacred souls who surrounded me—and my separation and soon to be divorce—precisely what my intentions were: I was not going for the jugular vein, and I will always love, honor, and support my soon-to-be ex-husband for who he is and for what he enabled me to become.

So, ask yourself how you would like to achieve the best possible situation and outcome, not only for yourself, but for everyone surrounding you and your situation of separation/divorce. Will you fall into the desperation and fear of attachment or will you embrace your situation with the grace and beauty of acceptance, taking decisive and responsible action based on nourishing choices and relinquishing all fear of judgment and of expectation? We should feel absolutely no need to defend our actions or ourselves, because we are part of the *divine* plan.

The spiritual essence of today activates the second chakra, also known as the svadhishthana chakra or creative chakra. It is located approximately three inches below the naval and is where all of our desires of creating actually manifest. It is where we have the intention of reading, writing, cooking, gardening, painting, sculpting, making the most exquisite music, and making the most divine and sacred love to our beloved. It is where babies come from, the unmanifest into the most glorious manifestation of life. This chakra is penetrated with a luminous, vibrant orange and resonates the healing vibration of *vam*. Please take a moment to sit in a cross-legged position, if comfortable. Close your eyes and take a deep breath in through your nostrils. Slowly and gently exhale the sound *vam*.

There is also a very empowering yoga posture known as Uttpluthi, the uplifting yoga pose that activates the svadhishthana chakra. This sacred little gem of a pose will strengthen your wrists, elbows, upper arms, and shoulders, as well as build immense abdominal strength. In addition to these exquisite toning effects, Uttpluthi will help in the prevention of Carpal Tunnel Syndrome. As with common sense, please consult the advice of a physician before engaging in any of the yoga poses instructed in this book. Begin by sitting in either the full Padmasana or Half Padmasana (Lotus, Tuesday's yoga pose). Next, raise the legs up, just a bit, toward the chest. Place your hands directly underneath each thigh, palms facing the floor. Inhale deeply, then exhale as you raise your entire body up and off of the floor. Are you levitating yet? Focus on a dristhi (a focal point in front of you) and lose yourself in this pose, with your breath. When you are ready to come out of it, simply bring your buttocks back to the floor and unfold your legs into a straight position. Please take the time to pamper yourself by massaging your thighs, knees, calves, arches of your feet, and your toes.

Photograph by Jasper Johal

"UTTPLUTHI UPLIFTING POSE"

I will now leave you for the day with this short but very powerful poem by Kabir: the profound mysticism of the Sufis, infused with the internal brilliance of the bhaktas, manifested into the most brilliant vineyard of poetic justice. His works are so profound that it feels as if they were part of his cellular functioning! He continues to be greatly revered in the universe of writing.

Seeking

Why run around sprinkling holy water? There's an ocean inside you, and when you're ready

You'll drink.

Self-Reflection Page

Please take a moment as you retire for the evening. Sitting comfortably in your bed, begin to journal your day. How was your day? How are you feeling physically, emotionally, and spiritually, right now? Let us begin the beautiful process of recapitulation. Remember, the joy is the very journey itself. Namaste.

Chapter Five: Thursday

Daily affirmation to tear out and carry with you throughout your day:

My intentions to manifest a peaceful outcome with my separation/divorce are completely supported by divine wisdom and protection.

Thursday

The wisdom of today graces us with the seeds of desire. If we harness these seeds with the utmost of integrity, all of our intentions in these desires will be completely and totally supported through divine principal. This then assures us of a peaceful outcome in every situation that we encounter, because we are simply surrendering to a higher purpose in life. We begin to realize that the single most important task we must accomplish in life is to love one another. We then realize that every intention and desire was originally born of universal truth.

How do we find out what universal truth is? And, when we find it, what do we do with it?

One way to discover what our true and real intentions and desires are is to meditate. Meditation is the single most effective way to find out, instantaneously, what you need in life and who you really are.

We find out who we truly are by letting our guard down through the release of stress that meditation brings. Stress is that obstruction in the pathway of our intentions and desires. When we experience stress, we manifest a number of physiological changes, such as:

- Increased heart rate
- Increased blood pressure

- Increased breathing
- Increased stress hormone release
- Sweating (and I am not referring to those pleasurable moments drenched in tantric rapture!)
- Weakened immunity
- Clotting of blood platelets

Yuck! Who needs this?

During the process of meditation, we shift our body into a divine state of restful awareness, which then manifests:

- Decreased heart rate
- Normalization of blood pressure
- Quiet, relaxed breathing
- Reduced stress hormones
- Reduced sweating
- Strengthened immunity

Now, that's more like it!

I mentioned in a previous chapter that when we pray, we talk to God. When we meditate, God talks to us. We only need to listen. This can be accessed more easily than you think. When we begin to meditate, our body begins to relax and our mind begins to relinquish all of the fifty to eighty thousand thoughts that run through our brain each and every day of our lives. We then relax so much that we enter into a very profound state where we are not thinking any thoughts, and in Chopra meditation, we are not thinking our mantra. We unite with divine love. It is here that we receive insight and guidance from God. God talks directly to us. We refer to this sacred union with the divine as "slipping into the gap." It is one of the most nourishing experiences you may manifest into your life. It is where you truly find out what it is that you are looking for. You discover what your intentions and desires really are. It is the place where you discover who you ultimately are.

What *are* your intentions and desires in your situation of separation and divorce? In contemplating this question, we must ask ourselves what it is that we truly wish to see fulfilled. What do we wholeheartedly desire to become manifest reality? What will we do with these desires once we have obtained them? What if what we initially wished for did not go precisely the way that we had planned it to go? What if universal spirit saw the motive of the intention and desire (with the best interest of *all* involved) and *blessed* you with something even grander than what you initially asked for? This is one of those "A-ha!" moments in our lives, having complete faith in every moment in life, knowing that this situation is for the best and that this journey is what we need to be on at this moment in life. Each and every situation that we encounter brings us one step closer to that sacred pathway to the journey of love. When we encounter an obstacle in life, we are really encountering a marvelous opportunity to reach out with love and change the course of action! It's true! Each and every one of us has the divine power to sail smoothly, even through the most turbulent of waters, by embracing the force and by moving *with* it. If you have ever been caught swimming in the ocean with a riptide, you will know precisely what I am referring to. When this situation happens, it works against the laws of nature. Unfortunately, some individuals fall victim and begin to struggle *against* the tide, vigorously and haphazardly exhausting every bit of energy left in them as they try to make it back to shore. When the body is found washed up on shore, "drowning" is the final diagnosis. Once again, another sad but very real statistic. In situations like this one, some people get so very frightened and consumed by fear that the ocean literally swallows them alive. The same exact energy is found in each and every separation and divorce. Knowing this ahead of time will not only save you precious time and money, but also your precious energy. This will convert it into more productive and fulfilling uses. When you are caught up in one of the many riptides of separation and divorce, try working *with* the energy instead of *against* it. The results will astound you, because you will achieve all of your intentions and desires naturally, without struggle or force. They will be supported by the universal principal of divine love. This principal of communication with the divine is accessed through the practice of meditation.

The choices are quite clear. Will you choose to be caught up in the riptide of hell, manifesting emotional, physical, and spiritual illness to yourself and all of those around you? Or will you consciously make all of your intentions and desires with peace, harmony, laughter, and love, blessing everyone around you with grace and divine principal? This alone will gift you with assurance. You will feel assured that all of your needs, physical, emotional, and spiritual, will be taken care of.

The spiritual essence of today activates the third chakra, also known as the manipura chakra. It is located in the solar plexus region of our body and is where all of our intentions and desires become the seeds of conscious manifestation. The color that radiates from this region of personal power is a bright and luminous yellow, and it commands the determined vibration *ram*. Please take a moment to sit in a cross-legged position, if comfortable. Close your eyes and take a deep breath in through your nostrils. Slowly and gently exhale the powerful sound *ram*.

There is also a deeply restorative yoga pose that will activate the manipura chakra. It is one of the most detoxifying yoga postures, as it releases accumulated toxins from the liver and the kidneys. It is known as Matsyandrasana, the seated spinal twist. Although this is considered to be a restorative yoga pose, it is not intended for individuals who have hip injuries or have had a hip replacement surgery. As with common sense, please consult the advice of a physician before engaging in any of the yoga poses instructed in this book. Begin by sitting on the floor with your legs straight out in front of you. Physically shift the flesh from the buttocks out to each side. With your hands, tip the pelvis up and then down. Bend your right knee, bringing your right foot as close to your right thigh as possible. Next, cross your right foot over your straight left leg and wrap your left leg around you, flexing your left foot and positioning it as close to your body as possible. Next, lower your left shoulder as you reach your left arm straight out to the side and wrap it around your crossed right leg. Gently hold onto your right thigh with your left hand. Now, lower your right shoulder and stretch your right arm out to the side and then straight up to the ceiling. Sit up as tall as you can, trying to get your arm as close to your ear as possible. Reach your right arm up and behind you, and rest the palm of your right hand on the floor. When you feel you have your position, twist your head over to the right and breathe. If you would like to intensify this pose, you may take the outside of your left elbow and gently rest it just above your right knee. Please sit up straight and tall. Enjoy your breath and feel the energy manifest harmony at a deep, cellular level. Matsyendrasana will lengthen the spine. It will massage and strengthen the liver and the kidneys and will stretch out your chest and shoulders.

When you are ready to come out of this pose, it is very important to compliment this pose with an alternative, spinal stretch. To come out, inhale then exhale as you release the pose, bringing your straight arms out to the right side first, then moving the straight arms in front of you and then over to your left side. Lower your arms as you then rest both hands on the floor on the left side of your body. The hands need to be placed slightly wider than shoulder-width apart, with the fingers pointed away from your body. Next, lower your shoulders as you bring your elbows straight out to the side. Then lower your head to the floor and breathe. When coming out of this complimentary stretch, simply lean your upper body back into a seated position. Please repeat (starting from the very beginning) this process on your left side. Feel the stretch compliment your prior stretch. The benefits of yoga are very precise, totally and completely manifesting deep relaxation and an amazing release of stress.

Photograph by Jasper Johal

"MATSYANDRASANA SEATED SPINAL TWIST"

I will now leave you with "The Sculptor," a poem written by the great Rabindranth Tagore. Its words, I promise you, are the very reflection of the spiritual essence of your intentions and desires to come. The world is indeed the oyster and *you* are the pearl. Namaste.

The Sculptor

When I thought to make your image
So people could worship it,
I molded it from my dust and desires,
Colored with delusion and dreaming.
Then I asked you to make an image of me
That you could love,
And you molded it from your own stuff:
Fire and might, truth, beauty and peace.

Self-Reflection Page

Please take a moment as you retire for the evening. Sitting comfortably in your bed, begin to journal your day. How was your day? How are you feeling physically, emotionally, and spiritually, right now? Let us begin the beautiful process of recapitulation. Remember, the joy is the very journey itself. Namaste.

Chapter Six: Friday

Daily affirmation to tear out and carry with you throughout your day:

I embrace uncertainty with the acceptance of grace, completely living in the freedom of detachment from any outcome of any situation I encounter in life.

Friday

The spiritual essence of today reflects the unknown field of pure potentiality. When we are truly present in the moment, we see the importance of uncertainty. We have access to an infinity of choices being presented to us and do not feel obligated to attach ourselves to any particular outcome. In the realm of detachment, we actually grace ourselves (and all of those around us) with the freedom of infinite possibilities.

Separation and divorce can be a virtual nightmare if we permit ourselves to be caught up in all of the drama. Today's words of wisdom guide us to simply detach from all of the accusations, lies, judgments, expectations, fears, interrogations, and every hideous, self-inflicted repository of human degradation one can conjure up. It's true! We make the choice to take on all of the drama and strife! For what? Why should we subject ourselves to such violent acts of hatred? Why even go there to begin with? We are not here to be the doormat for the Roman Empire' to smear their emotional grime of ego-inflated, disgusting vulgarity on. We simply have no other choice. We cannot embrace hatred by being passive. In the same vein, we also must not fight with negative energy. By simply detaching from all of the turmoil and chaos, we achieve maximum results! Do whatever you need to do to make yourself unavailable for the drama. Let it go! Let the universe handle every detail in your intentions of peace, harmony, laughter, and love.

When we allow ourselves to not get caught up in the potential drama that a separation and divorce can bring, we then open up a whole new realm of infinite possibilities. By remaining uncertain of the outcome, we then discover that harmonious solutions to our situations in our separation and divorce will naturally be revealed. The clouds of turmoil, anguish, and strife will miraculously begin to lift. The fog of hatred will dissipate as the quality of our intentions and desires of manifesting a peaceful separation/peaceful divorce become a reality. It will be a conscious reality based on simply letting yourself and everyone and every situation that surrounds your separation/ divorce simply *be*. You relinquish the need to fix all of the problems in your case (and in the case of your soon-to-be ex-betrothed). Sometimes, when we take on the role of life's carpenter, we may neglect to enforce the structured plans with a support beam, resulting in emotional crash and burn, only making matters worse! We must let it go. We must let it be.

Furthermore, we don't need to reach a settlement to feel exonerated. It is when we truly detach from the outcome that we marvel in the freedom of liberation. The origins of liberation stem from the moment we take the time to let it be.

John Lennon and Paul McCartney's beautifully poignant song clearly illustrated, with sheer poetic justification, how very real we must remain in the field of detachment. The entire song is nothing short of a miracle. It even grasps the magnitude of what Christ's teachings were all about. There is one profound phrase that speaks directly into the eyes of what we are going through as individuals of separation and divorce. "And when the broken-hearted people living in the world agree, there will be an answer. Let it be. For though they may be parted there is still a chance that they will see. There will be an answer. Let it be."

In the passionately exquisite writings of Elizabeth Cunningham's absolutely, incredible book, *The Passion of Mary Magdalene*, she captured a moment in time and held it in the visshuddha chakra of Mary Magdalene. Elizabeth writes of Joseph (a friend of Mary's and also of Jesus') speaking with Mary:

"My dear," he said after a time, "you do know that Jesus is in danger."

"So, what else is new?"

"I'm serious, Maeve. Jesus is Herod's new nightmare, now that John is dead, *because* John is dead."

"Joanna—she's the wife of Herod's steward—she predicted as much," I said.

"I know for a fact, never mind how, that Herod has sent out spies to track him. And it's not just Herod who's keeping an eye on him. Word has spread about whatever happened on the hillside that night—no, I don't want to hear about any more miracles; it makes me queasy. Anyway, it doesn't matter. The powers that be, Roman and Jewish, know he could raise an army. If he chose."

"But he doesn't want an army," I said. "He refused to marshal people that way."

"What does he want, Maeve? What does he think he's doing?"

"He, he wants to…" And I realized with a shock, I couldn't answer.

"Well, couldn't you talk your husband into keeping a low profile for a while?"

"Sure, and while I'm at it, I'll ask him to reverse the sun's direction and have the mountains change places with the sea."

Mary Magdalene clearly had no other choice than to detach. She loved Jesus so much that she *had* to let it be.

*The spiritual essence of today activates the fifth chakra, also known as the visuddha chakra. It is located in the region of the throat, and it is where personal expression resides. There is an exquisite and ethereal light blue that seems to transcend through this chakra, and it has a most melodic and harmonious hymn of a vibrational sound. It is *ham*. Please take a moment to sit in a cross-legged position, if comfortable. Close your eyes and take a deep breath in through your nostrils. Slowly and gently surrender your exhalation to the healing vibration of *ham*.

There is also a magnificent yoga posture to activate the visuddha chakra. A restorative posture that offers many medical benefits, Setu Bandhasana, often referred to as the bridge pose, has a deep variation that can be quite liberating indeed! For my female readers, please enjoy this yoga posture when you are not menstruating, as your body needs this time for cleansing and renewal. As with common sense, please consult the advice of a physician before engaging in any of the yoga poses instructed in this book. Begin by lying down on your back with your knees bent and your feet resting flat on the floor, slightly wider than hip-width apart. With your feet securely pressed into the floor, inhale deeply. As you exhale, lower the spine, tip your pelvis upward, squeeze the buttocks, and begin to raise your hips and buttocks up toward the ceiling. Relax your jaw, making sure that it is not jammed into your chest. Then, press the shoulders into the floor as you reach both of your arms behind your back. Clasp both hands together as if in a prayer pose and press the entire length of both arms and hands into the floor. Focus on a dristhi, on the ceiling, as you squeeze your thighs, buttocks, and calves. Don't forget to breathe! When you want to detach from this pose, inhale as you slowly release your arms and lower your spine and buttocks back down to the floor. Setu Bandhasana will strengthen your thyroid as it stretches out your neck, spine, shoulders, and chest. In addition, it will stimulate the kidneys and liver, improving your digestion. It also relieves symptoms of menopause. Pretty cool stuff, for sure!

I had the profound honor of posing for the renowned spiritual artist Paul Heussenstamm in an intensified variation of Setu Bandhasana. It is the first nude yoga painting ever manifested. When I was posing, it felt as if all of the yogis and yoginis of the past transcended through me. It was not a painting of sexual exploration; rather it was of the complete and total acceptance that one has when one is absolutely detached from the yoga posture itself, delving into the sacred union with the divine through the breath. It was truly enlightening. If you would like to view this painting, it may be seen on Paul's Web site, www.mandalas.com.

Photograph by Jasper Johal

"SETU BANDHASANA BRIDGE POSE"

I shall leave you for the day to reflect the timeless grace of Rumi and his very eloquent poem.

Lost in the Wilderness

Oh lovers!
Where are you going?
Who are you looking for?
Your beloved is right here.
She lives in your own neighborhood.
Her face is veiled.
She hides behind screens
calling for you
while you search and lose yourself
in the wilderness and the desert.
Cease looking for flowers!
There blooms a garden in your own home
While you look for trinkets
the treasure house awaits you in your own being.
There is no need for suffering.
God is here.

Self-Reflection Page

Please take a moment as you retire for the evening. Sitting comfortably in your bed, begin to journal your day. How was your day? How are you feeling physically, emotionally, and spiritually, right now? Let us begin the beautiful process of recapitulation. Remember, the joy is the very journey itself. Namaste.

Chapter Seven: Saturday

Daily affirmation to tear out and carry with you throughout your day:

I am a divine spiritual being, and I harmonize my life by doing what it is that I love to do while serving those around me through peaceful, harmonious, light-hearted, and loving actions.

Saturday

The spiritual essence of today graces us with the infinite. Our soul is timeless, and today, we take the time to ignite the infinite flame of passion that resides deep within our soul. We realize why we are actually here. This realization is obtained by serving all of those around us with every single passion that ignites our heart. Our separation and divorce is not an ending. It is not extinguishing our passionate flame in life. Rather, it is a release. This release will ignite that passionate, infinite flame that resides deep within us, just waiting to serve everyone *with peace, harmony, laughter, and* love.

"You're *not* giving up on your dream, *Mom*! I won't let you! You absolutely *cannot* give up your *dharma*!"

Ah, yes, out of the mouth of babes. My incredible eleven-year-old daughter has already been graced with sagelike wisdom and profound spirituality.

She was adamantly advising me to hold tight to my dream and not let anything get in the way of my passions, intentions, and desires. You see, when we share our deepest desires with individuals who truly care for us, the apostles in our mission, all that we desire will become universally supported.

In this particular case, my daughter actually assisted me every step of the way in the process of becoming certified to instruct primordial sound meditation, the timeless and sacred practice of Chopra meditation. I had been studying for two years, and the time had come. I passed all of my pre-exams and was ready to embark on the certification process in this amazing and fulfilling journey.

It was a bright and cheerful summer afternoon. I wrapped up teaching several yoga sessions in Malibu and headed back into the city with my car all packed up and ready for the adventure that would change my life forever. I was, however, completely unaware that the universe was going to present me with a challenge that would eventually enforce my dharma with incredible passion and determination.

When I arrived in the city to pick up my daughter and my mother, the excitement of love and support filled every part of my being. Both my daughter and my mother were so happy for me and were eager to witness this accomplishment in my life. This kind of unconditional love is one of the greatest moments anyone can have.

Arriving at La Costa is always a beautiful and welcoming experience. Being greeted with genuine and heartfelt hugs at the Chopra Center, which is in La Costa, always feels like coming home to family on holidays.

The journey was beginning. Both my daughter and my mother were basking in the lasting bonds of their relationship as I began the training and testing phase in becoming a meditation teacher. The week was unfolding beautifully. Then it happened.

My very dear friend, Alma, phoned to inform me that her teenage daughter (who was taking care of our dogs while we were away) came into my home to find my soon-to-be ex-husband's (his name is George) girlfriend and her son hanging out in my home! Yes, it's true. George had given the key to my home to his present girlfriend. Imagine this!

I instantaneously felt all of the physiological changes of the fight/flight response that occurs when one is stressed out. I became one with

- Increased heart rate
- Increased blood pressure
- Increased breathing
- Increased stress hormone release
- Sweating
- Weakened immunity
- Clotting of blood platelets

Yes, I was indeed *pissed off*.

What is one to do in this case? Well, I was ready to pack it all up and leave. I was willing to let the stress of the moment consume my purpose in life and relinquish every passion in fulfilling my dharma. I was done—or so I thought.

Then my precious daughter held me in her loving embrace, gazed into my eyes, and, with both of her tiny hands holding onto my face, said, "You're *not* giving up on your dream, *Mom*! I won't let you! You absolutely *cannot* give up your *dharma*!" It rekindled that spark of passion deep within my soul and began to ignite it with renewed strength, courage, and complete determination.

My mother also gave me her undivided love and support, and when I returned after a very profound and meditative walk, I was embraced wholeheartedly by those incredible souls that make the Chopra Center the healing Mecca of the universe.

This was the most incredible example of unconditional love and support. Their support was authentic. It was real, and it was alive.

I went back and finished the testing and training portion of this program. As I glanced back to see the love and support beaming in the eyes of my daughter and my mother, I received my diploma with deep appreciation and grace.

This was one of those moments in life where I have never felt more a part of God, have never borne witness to that very powerful goddess that resides deep inside of my integral being. There was nothing that would ever stop me. Not one single thing will ever get in my way again. I realize who I am, and I am fully aware of what I must accomplish in life. My dharma is the will of God, and I will fulfill every aspect of it!

This situation that I just informed you of is a clear example of an obstacle in the pathway of our intentions and desires. Had I left and gone back to the stress of this situation, it would have accomplished absolutely nothing. It would have caused resentment, neglect, guilt, anger, frustration—all of it.

Every stressful situation that occurs in each and every one of our lives gives us two choices. Do we allow the situation to consume us or do we detach from the drama, remaining in our own field of pure potentiality, which will then manifest infinite possibilities of endless pleasure?

Pleasure, true and unbridled happiness, is derived from our soul, fulfilling a purpose and serving humanity with this purpose. This, ultimately, is the reason why we are here: to love and help one another.

Seek and ye shall find. Knock and the door will be opened. Who *are* you? What do you want? What *are* your deepest desires? How will you serve humanity with these desires? How determined *are* you to manifest the outcome of these desires? These are all questions of the soul. Our soul's purpose lies far beyond our immediate concerns and demands.

If we take the time to lovingly nourish our soul with these questions, we then allow the soul to discover who we really are and what it is that we really must accomplish while we are here on this earth.

Likewise, if we allow ourselves to be caught up in the immediate demands of stressful situations, we allow the ego to extinguish the flame of passion that resides deep inside of our intentions and desires, completely sabotaging our soul's purpose in life.

The ego resides not in universal consciousness. Rather, it thrives in the field of judgment and expectation and chaos. It concerns itself with only the self and nothing else.

Have you ever been on a date with someone who is physically beautiful? Then, suddenly you realize that every single word that they are saying feels like a bad script in a vulgar play? You see that they would be much happier actually conversing into a mirror, as they are so absorbed in their own self that they have simply lost sight of any form of real human connection. You are trying so very desperately not to be rude when glancing at your watch, as precious time is stolen every moment wasted with this individual. Man, I would rather have the flu than endure any more of those encounters. I did it once and my lesson was learned!

Then, we discover that there is so much more to our body, mind, and soul. We find a real need to connect with a greater purpose, a greater truth, a more genuine reality of higher states of consciousness.

We then begin to manifest in our lives those sacred beings that are real. They are deeply authentic. They have a purpose in life, and they know who they are. They are helping to heal the universe, and they are making a difference in the world.

We, each and every one of us, have this access. It is easier to obtain than perhaps you realize. It is done through the regular practice of yoga and meditation. It happens when we take the time to quiet the mind. Then we access these higher states of our soul and unite collectively with the universal intentions and desires just waiting to unfold into our lives.

During meditation, we receive divine guidance for fulfilling and harnessing all of our desires and serving humanity, the animal kingdom, and the planet. Not for us, but for *all* of us combined as a whole and living entity of divine consciousness, uniting with universal spirit. It is the purest form of existence, and there is simply nothing more important right now than to accomplish this level of consciousness.

In separation and divorce, we can become clouded with the fog of insecurity and fear. This fog has the capacity to completely block out the intentions and desires of our dharma. Our dharma is then replaced with drama. We get caught up in the super inflated egos of our attorneys.

I certainly do appreciate the need for a legal approach to separation and to divorce, and encourage you to find out *who* you really are and *what* you really want *before* you even permit someone else to govern your body, your mind, and ultimately, your soul.

In simply divine words, you are your soul, the purest form of divine love. Your body is the temple and your mind is the direct link to God. This link is connected through meditation and through prayer. We connect in this silent space, where we discover what our mission is and how to handle the inevitable stressful situations that arise in a separation and divorce. It is here where we obtain the strength that we need to endure even the harshest of situations.

When we encounter these stressful situations in a separation and divorce, we *must* gift ourselves with precious time. Even a brief moment to be still and sitting in a comfortable position and breathing. Releasing all thoughts, relinquishing all demands, and surrendering to the healing silence that meditation graces you with will bring you peace. The benefits of living peacefully, even in the midst of chaos, will grace you with time to reflect. It is this precious time that we gift ourselves with that will enable us to make the spontaneous, correct, karmic decision at any given point during our transition from being married to being separated and divorced. Time spent in meditation and prayer instead of in a lawyer's office will ultimately be your pocket watch to a peaceful outcome in your situation.

Remember, I appreciate the value of good, solid legal advice, especially when it comes from the heart. I am simply advising you to be totally and completely centered before you even step foot in the legal doorway.

Only you know what is in your best interest and in the best interest of everyone involved in your separation and divorce. The self-realization that *you* are your *soul* and your body is the *house* for it will assure your mind that all of your choices will be the correct ones for you and your loved ones. Only *you* know what is best for your *house*. How you wish to design it, from the tranquil, serenity inside to the flourishing garden outside, is entirely up to you.

Realizing that your body is housing your soul, you should never cloud your *house* with someone else's interpretations of how it should look or rather (to put it bluntly) sell on the market. Your soul is not of market value and must never be sold.

You are that sacred and infinite being residing in that beautiful *house*. Deep inside of your soul lies a god or goddess just waiting to manifest your dharma—just waiting to transform your *house* into the most glorious universal palace. In the sheer glory of this transformation, your soul will thrive, and you will live in a continuous state of bliss. The god or goddess will awaken and guide you to your appropriate resources.

You have picked up this book for a reason. This reason is your resource. This reason is your strength. Only you know how to find out why. Only you know what this reason is, and only you will ensure the outcome of your separation and divorce.

Take the time today to appreciate that precious part of you that lies deep within your soul. You are a part of the divine plan. You are a part of collective consciousness. You are a part of universal truth, and you are a part of God.

The spiritual essence of today activates the sixth chakra, also known as the ajna chakra. It is located between the eyebrows and assists us in providing insight and intuition. The exquisite color of indigo radiates through this chakra region, and it has a clarifying sound of *sham*. Please sit in a comfortable, cross-legged position, if possible. Close your eyes and breath in deeply, feeling this beautiful indigo color penetrate your ajna chakra. Now, slowly exhale the healing sound *sham*. Feel the connection of your body as it unites with your mind, connecting to your soul. Feel the complete feeling of bliss. Feel the union.

There is also an amazing and graceful yoga posture that activates the ajna chakra. It strengthens the lower back, as well as the kidneys and liver. It also stretches the front of the thighs, chest, and neck, and firms the buttocks. It is the exquisite Chakrasana, the kneeling wheel pose. It can be quite a liberating asana to incorporate into your practice. This posture is not intended for those individuals with a recent knee injury or surgical procedures. As with common sense, please consult the advice of a physician before engaging in any of the yoga poses instructed in this book.

Please begin by kneeling with your knees hip-width apart, as your upper body extends to a position that is straight and tall. Roll your shoulders up, around to the back, then down. Next, please place your hands together and rest them on your chest, close to the sternum. Close your eyes, take a deep breath in, and take a moment to appreciate the grace and beauty that resides deep within your soul. Exhale. Next, extend your right arm straight out in front of you as you reach out and grasp your right ankle with your right hand. Please notice that the palm of your right hand should be facing the right side of your surroundings as it holds onto the inner portion of the arch of your right foot. Now repeat this same exact procedure on your left side. Next, begin arching your back as you raise your hips upward. Squeeze the buttocks and breathe. Surrender to the healing sound of your breath. In addition to the medical benefits, as you engage fully into this pose, forming the shape of the wheel, it will activate each chakra region, providing incredible strength and renewed energy.

Photograph by Jasper Johal

"CHAKRASANA KNEELING WHEEL/CAMEL POSE"

I shall leave you with this divinely exquisite poem. Short and sweet and quite poetically poignant, Rumi's poem has captured the spiritual essence of today. Enjoy.

People want you to be happy.
Don't keep serving them your pain!
If you could untie your wings
and free your soul of jealousy,
You and everyone around you
would fly up like doves.

Self-Reflection Page

Please take a moment as you retire for the evening. Sitting comfortably in your bed, begin to journal your day. How was your day? How are you feeling physically, emotionally, and spiritually, right now? Let us begin the beautiful process of recapitulation. Remember, the joy is the very journey itself. Namaste.

Epilogue

As you make the journey from being married to being separated and divorced, be gentle with yourself. Take the time to pause, to reflect, and to embrace each and every day of the week. When we welcome each day with the spiritual essence that emanates from the universe, we then embrace each moment in our lives with grace.

This book is intended to be a source of strength for you as you make your transition. It is meant to be read and reread, again and again. You may wish to keep it on your bedside table and read a chapter each day, beginning on Sunday and concluding on a Saturday, allowing the spiritual essence to guide you, embrace you, and gently caress you in the palms of loving hands.

Surround yourself with loving support and individuals who truly nourish you and will be there for you, without a motive. You may choose to join a support group, join in a yoga class, or become part of a meditation group. Whatever means of emotional support you gravitate towards will be the most appropriate one for you at this point in your life.

Also know that you are not alone. Many people have gone through the pain and agony of a separation and divorce. Some have been bitter experiences and some have been more liberating. Each and every separation and divorce is different. Each and every one has the potential to create a peaceful and harmonious outcome.

Know that you are in charge. You are not going to be a victim. Know that all of your needs will be taken care of. The universe will never give you anything too tough for you to handle. You will see this through. Although the light at the end of that dark tunnel may appear to be faint or even non-existent at the moment, know that it will shine and become a radiant beam of pure potentiality once again.

Yoga and meditation will most definitely manifest a renewed strength into your life and will even guide you to infinite possibilities of peace, harmony, laughter, and love. Please take the time and find a local public class or inquire about taking private sessions, whether with a close friend or by simply enjoying the pleasure of your own company, carefully and lovingly instructed. The benefits are miraculous.

As a Chopra yoga and meditation instructor, I have had the profound honor to serve humanity with authentic grace and complete dedication. The results that I have witnessed have been miraculous, as I watched my beloved students journey that ultimate pathway to enlightenment. I continue to bask in awe at the profound gift to the universe, that Chopra instruction brings. It seems like we have been chosen to serve. We, wholeheartedly, are truly in this for service—to serve humanity with grace, with dignity, with the highest integrity, and with supreme love for *all*.

I also recommend that you attend one of the many beautifully healing seminars and workshops offered by the Chopra Center. Located in Carlsbad, California, the Chopra Center resides in the lovely surroundings at La Costa Resort and Spa. For more information on the various programs available, please visit www.Chopra.com.

One final note. Because I truly believe in serving humanity and in this mission, I will donate 10 percent of all of the proceeds of this book to the Alliance for a New Humanity. This is a beautiful and divinely guided non-profit organization, manifested by the remarkable Dr. Deepak Chopra. Its profound mission is to harness and sustain global peace, ecological balance and social justice. I believe we truly can make a difference. Deepak writes:

"At this moment, nothing is more important for healing the world than to link all those who believe that we must set forth a new narrative and create a new world where hope, social justice, peace, and a sense of the sacredness of life prevail. For this, we need to form a critical mass of humanity that influences change at a global scale, to bring together the inner streams of sensitive human beings."

Join us: www.deepakchopra.com

As you embrace the qualities of peace, harmony, laughter and love that reside deeply in your heart, you may find that a part of you has changed. If you are willing to make a commitment to keeping this positive shift of awareness alive, please visit www.itakethevow.com. Be the change!

Thank you for allowing me to serve you in a beautiful and loving way. Thank you, for embracing my words of wisdom and permitting them to nourish your body, your mind, and your soul. And, thank you, my precious reader, for your contribution to manifesting more peace, harmony, laughter, and love in this world. You are indeed very much appreciated.

I wish you much love and happiness and all of God's blessings.

Love always,
Heather

Photograph by Jasper Johal

About the Author

Known as the ultimate yoga instructor to many people in the film and music industries, Heather Frenner, a student of psychology, is a certified Chopra yoga instructor, a certified primordial sound meditation instructor, a Chopra Center ayurvedic products consultant, and a certified children's yoga instructor. She is certified with the Viritus Child Protection Training Program, holds a BRN and AAPA certificate in Continuing Medical Education from the University of California San Diego, and is registered with the elite Yoga Alliance and Yoga Journal.

Visit the author online at www.heatherfrenneryt.com.